The Big Little Golden Book of Planets

By Robert Bell

Illustrated by Tom LaPadula

A Golden Book • New York
Western Publishing Company, Inc., Racine, Wisconsin 53404

Copyright © 1987 by Robert Bell. Illustrations copyright © 1987 by Tom LaPadula. All rights reserved. Printed in the U.S.A. by Western Publishing Company, Inc. No part of this book may be reproduced or copied in any form without written permission from the publisher. GOLDEN®, GOLDEN & DESIGN®, A GOLDEN BOOK®, and A BIG LITTLE GOLDEN BOOK® are trademarks of Western Publishing Company, Inc. Library of Congress Catalog Card Number: 86-83065 ISBN: 0-307-10279-3/ISBN: 0-307-68279-X (lib. bdg.) A B C D E F G H I J K L M

The Publisher gratefully acknowledges the assistance of NASA in checking the scientific accuracy of this book.

Have you ever looked down at Earth from a mountain or an airplane? If you have, you have seen that Earth is a big place, much bigger than it looks from down below.

As big as it is, though, Earth isn't the only place.

If you look up into the sky, you see lights: the sun by day and the moon and stars by night. These lights are places, too—strange and wonderful places. Most of them are so far away that we cannot visit them. But even so, we know a lot about them.

The sun is the brightest light in our sky. It looks so bright because it is very hot and very big. The sun is 865,000 miles wide. A million of our Earths could fit inside it and there would still be room to spare. The sun is made up of gases and is 25 million degrees Fahrenheit in its center—50,000 times hotter than a burning match.

It is a good thing for us that the sun is so bright and hot. Every living thing on Earth needs the sun's light and warmth.

Nine planets circle the sun like horses on a merry-go-round. The sun and its planets together are called the solar system, and the sun is the biggest thing in it.

Earth, our home, is one of the nine planets. If you know where to look at night, you can see a few of the other planets among the stars. But most of the solar system's planets are too far away and too dim to see.

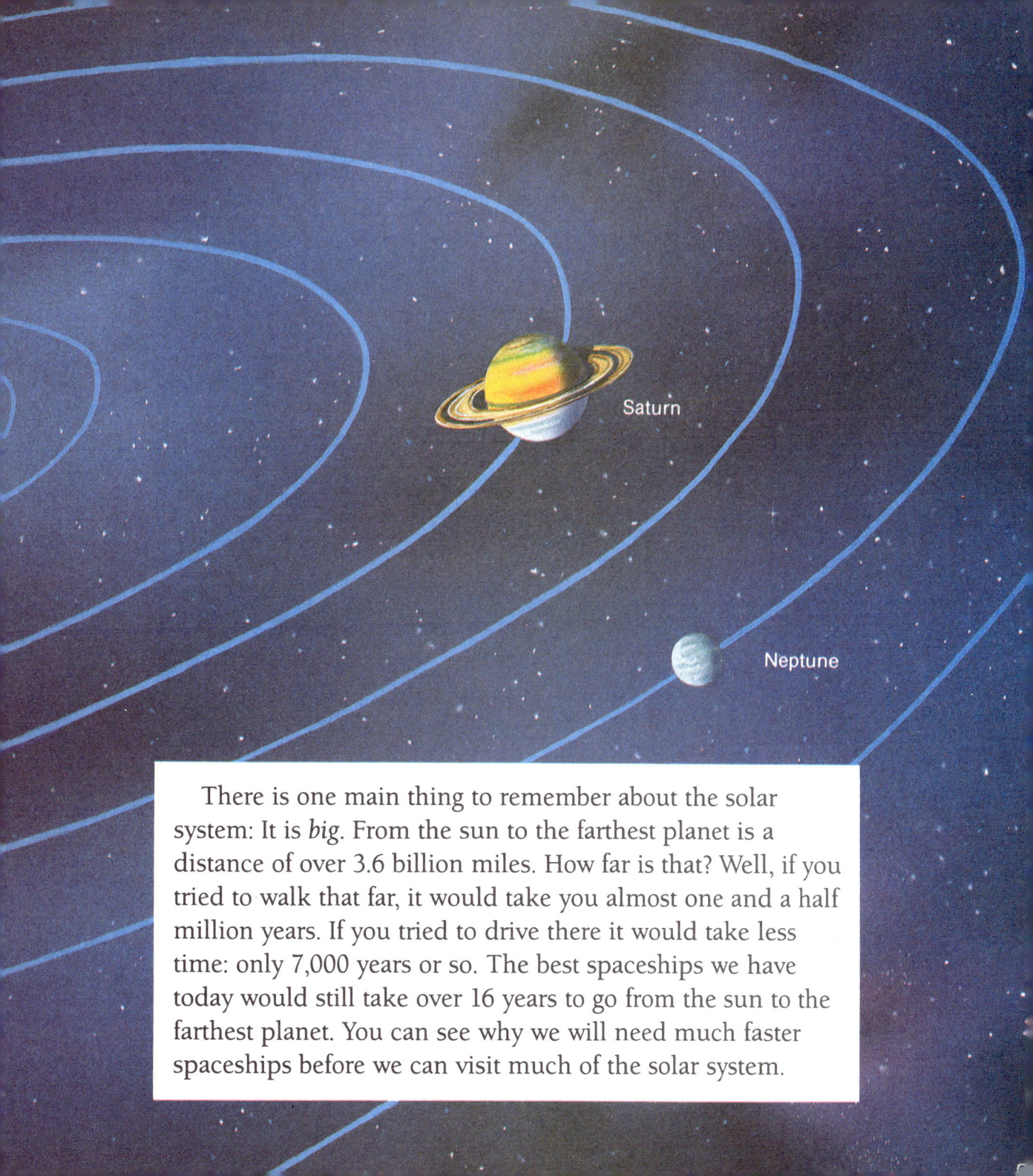

There is one main thing to remember about the solar system: It is *big*. From the sun to the farthest planet is a distance of over 3.6 billion miles. How far is that? Well, if you tried to walk that far, it would take you almost one and a half million years. If you tried to drive there it would take less time: only 7,000 years or so. The best spaceships we have today would still take over 16 years to go from the sun to the farthest planet. You can see why we will need much faster spaceships before we can visit much of the solar system.

The planet closest to the sun is Mercury. Mercury is also the smallest planet in the solar system. It is a ball of rock and dirt without any air or water. No plants grow there. Neither people nor animals live there.

If you stood on Mercury and looked up, the sun would be nine times bigger than it is in Earth's sky. That is because Mercury is so much closer to the sun.

Mercury is a very hot place because it is so near the sun. But it is a very cold place, too.

Have you ever noticed how it is always colder on Earth after the sun goes down than it is during the day? During the day on Mercury it gets more than hot enough to set this book on fire. But at night, when the sun is hidden, it gets more than twice as cold as Earth's coldest winter night.

The second planet in the solar system is Venus. It is very different from Mercury. For one thing, Venus has air. It is also wrapped in bright clouds, which make the planet bright enough for you to see at night among the stars.

What is underneath those clouds? It is not a place you would like very much. The air is poisonous. The clouds shut out all light but a dim red glow. And it is even hotter down there than on Mercury. The heavy clouds trap heat from the sun, with the same effect as a car with its windows closed on a hot summer day.

Like Mercury, Venus has no water, no plants, and no people. It is mostly a rocky desert. But there are some high mountains on Venus. The highest one, Maxwell Montes, is seven miles high, nearly two miles higher than Mount Everest, Earth's biggest mountain.

Earth is the third planet in the solar system. As far as we know, it is the only place in the solar system where plants grow and where animals and people live. Earth is at exactly the right distance from the sun for this—93 million miles.

Like all the planets, Earth travels around the sun in a big circle. Earth takes 365 days to make that circle. We call this period a year. Earth also spins like a top in space, just like all the other planets in the solar system. It takes Earth 24 hours to spin around once, and that's what we call a day.

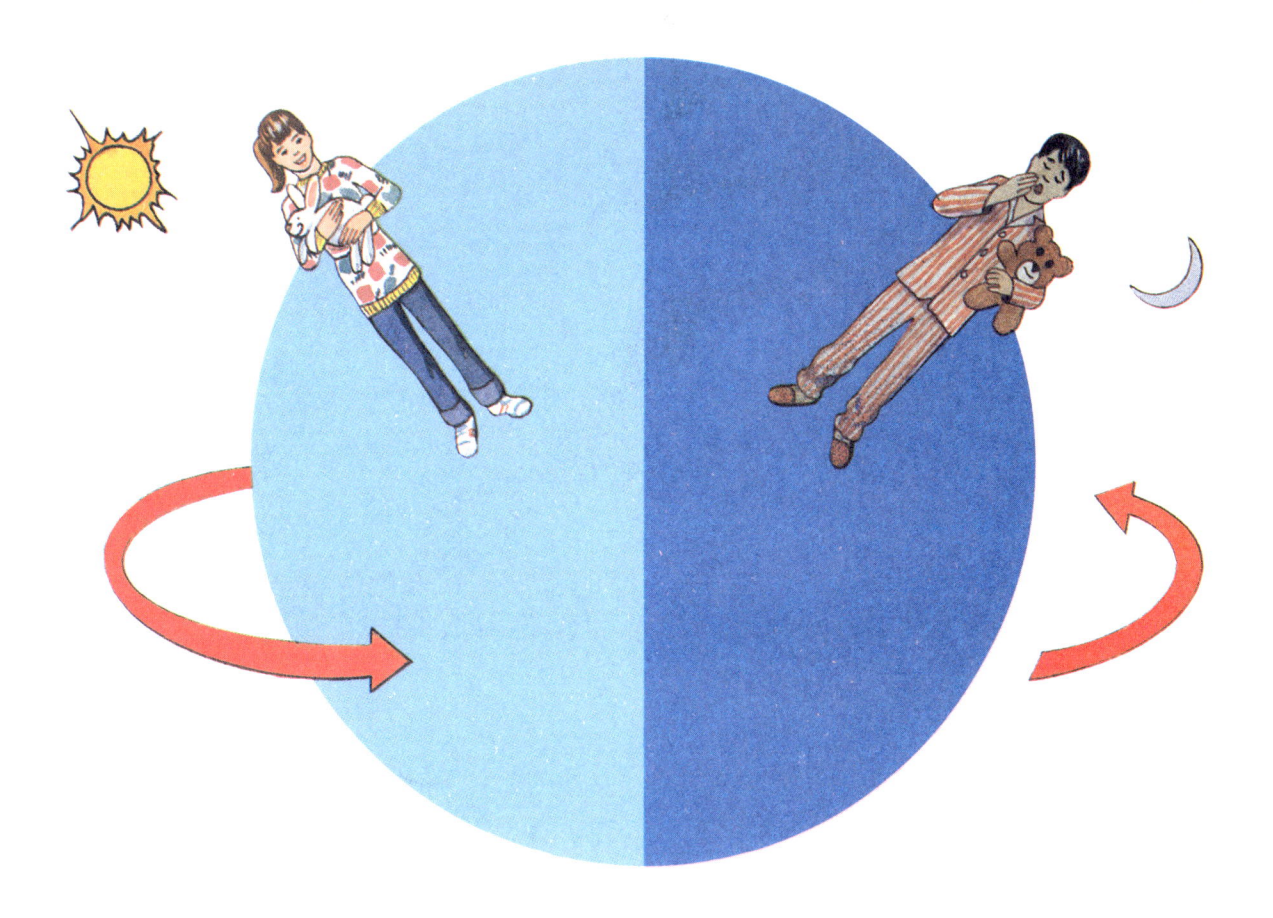

Have you ever wondered why there is day and night? The secret is in the way Earth spins. The sun lights only one side of Earth. The other side is in shadow. As Earth spins, your home moves gradually into shadow and then back into sunlight, into shadow and into sunlight, over and over again.

From your home it looks as though the sun rises in the east and moves across the sky to go down in the west. But the sun isn't moving; it is really Earth and everything on it that moves.

The brightest thing in the night sky is Earth's moon. Our moon travels around Earth in the same way the planets circle the sun. Our moon is so bright because it is our nearest neighbor in the solar system.

Earth is not the only planet with a moon. But we know more about our moon than we know about any other place in the solar system. American astronauts have made six trips there.

The moon is a lot like Mercury—a ball of rock and dirt without air, water, or life. When astronauts visited the moon, they had to bring their own food, water, and air. They had to wear special suits that contained air for them to breathe. And they had to return to Earth before their food, water, and air were all used up.

Deimos

The fourth planet in the solar system is Mars. The rock and dirt of Mars is rich in the reddish material we call rust. That is why Mars is known as the Red Planet.

Mars is the only planet besides Earth that has caps of ice at its North and South poles. Long ago, Mars also had rivers and streams. In fact, scientists once hoped that there were Martians—people who lived on Mars.

But we now know that Mars is a desert with air too thin for people to breathe. Winds blow and stir up huge storms of red dust. There are deep canyons and high mountains. One mountain on Mars, Mons Olympus, is even higher than the giant mountain on Venus. Mars' big mountain is over twice the size of Earth's tallest peak.

Mars has two moons, Deimos and Phobos. Both these tiny moons move fast. They circle Mars in hours instead of days.

Phobos

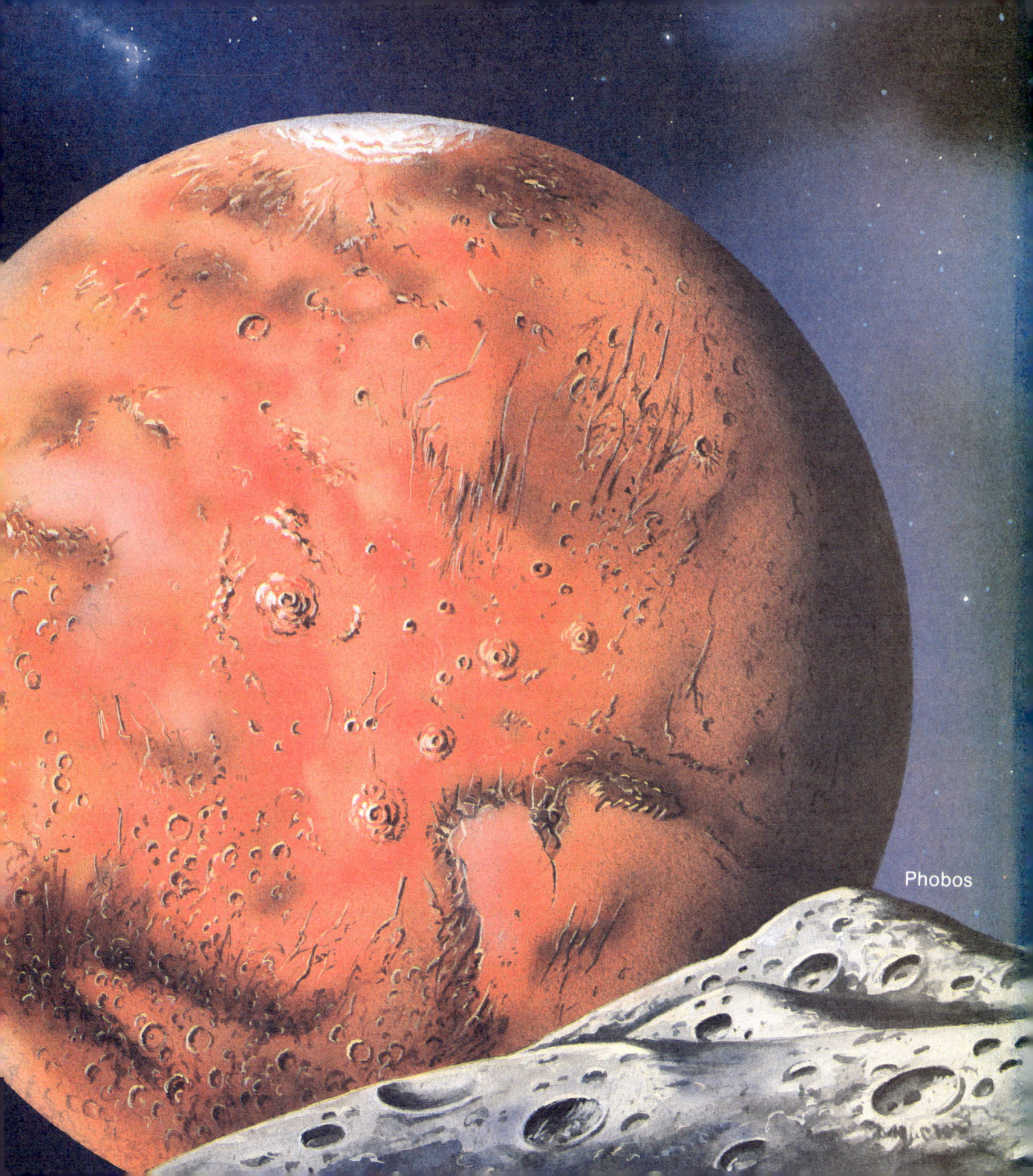

Jupiter is the fifth planet. Like Venus, it is completely covered by clouds.

But Jupiter is very different from Venus. For one thing, it is the biggest planet in the solar system. In fact, you could fit 1,300 Earths inside it.

Jupiter is different in another way, too. Under the clouds of Venus is a planet made of rock and dirt. Under Jupiter's clouds, though, is nothing but more clouds. Jupiter is a gigantic ball of colored gas, the first and biggest of the planets we call "gas giants."

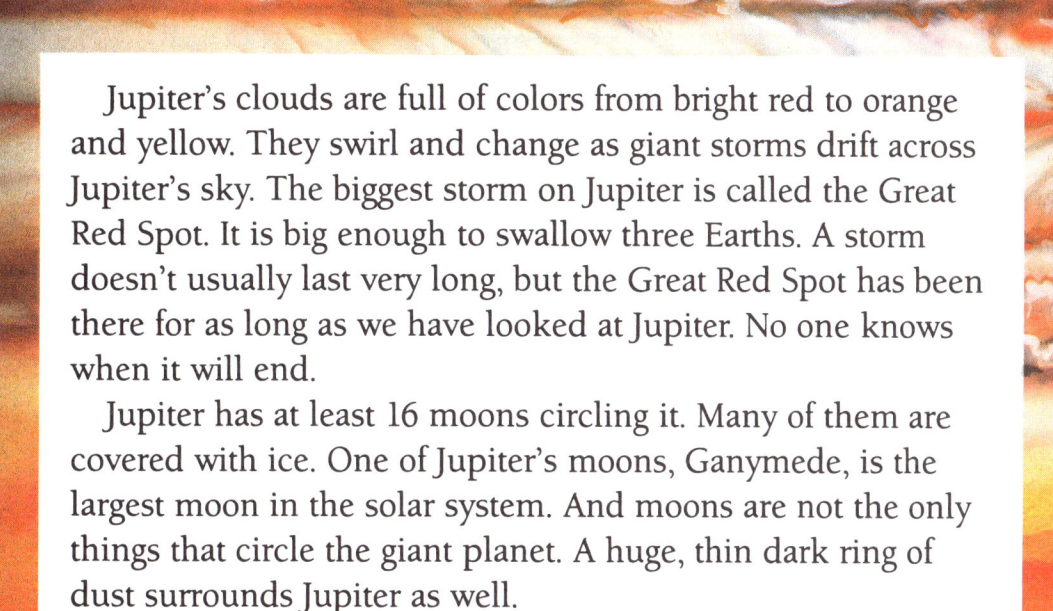

Jupiter's clouds are full of colors from bright red to orange and yellow. They swirl and change as giant storms drift across Jupiter's sky. The biggest storm on Jupiter is called the Great Red Spot. It is big enough to swallow three Earths. A storm doesn't usually last very long, but the Great Red Spot has been there for as long as we have looked at Jupiter. No one knows when it will end.

Jupiter has at least 16 moons circling it. Many of them are covered with ice. One of Jupiter's moons, Ganymede, is the largest moon in the solar system. And moons are not the only things that circle the giant planet. A huge, thin dark ring of dust surrounds Jupiter as well.

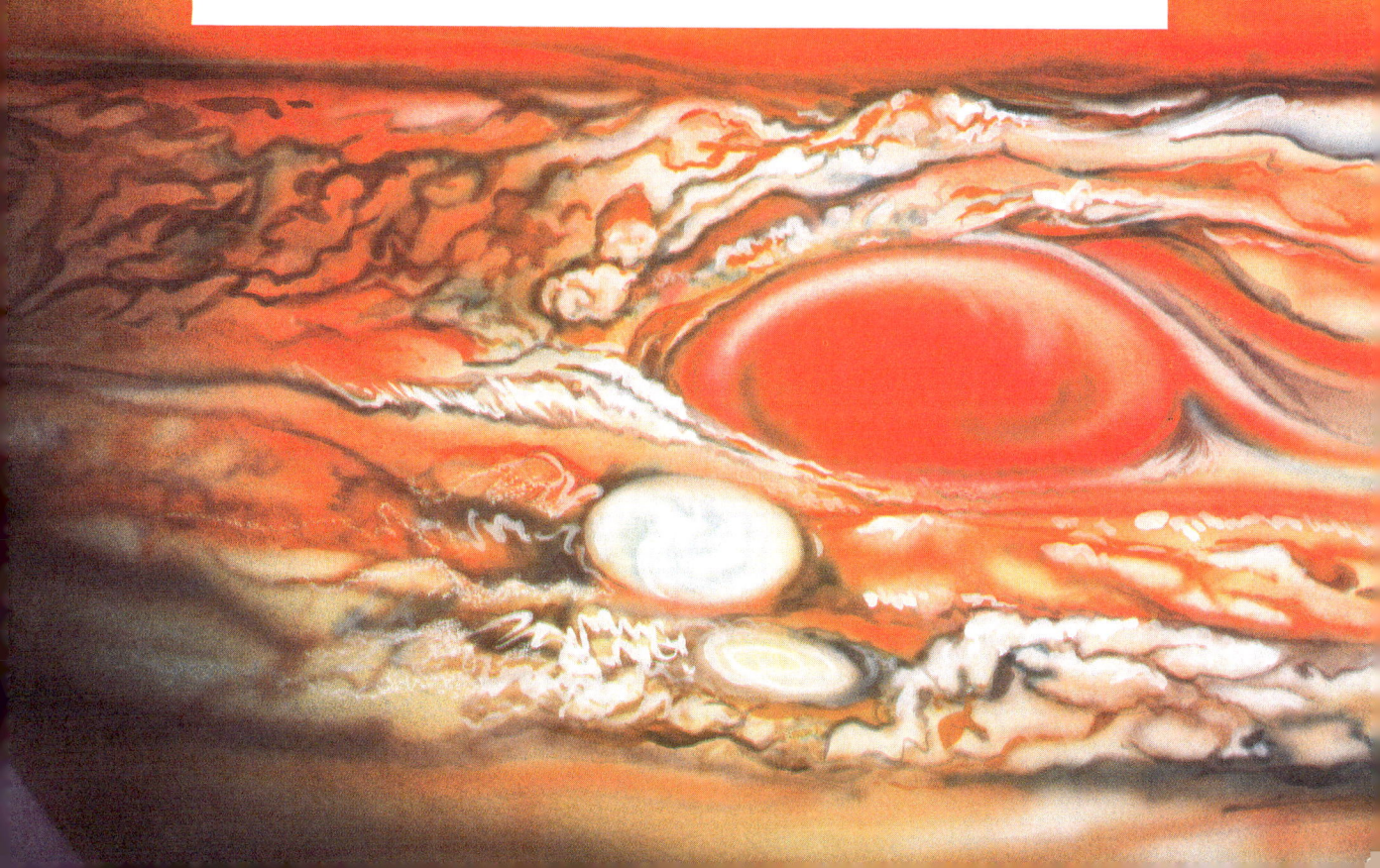

Saturn, the sixth planet, is also a gas giant. It is about half the size of Jupiter and is surrounded by rings. In fact, Saturn is known as the "ringed planet" because it has the biggest and most beautiful set of rings in the solar system.

The rings look solid enough to stand and walk on, but they are not. They are made up of millions of pieces of ice, rock, and dust circling Saturn together.

Saturn also has more moons than any other planet in the solar system. We have counted 23 of them so far.

One of these moons, Titan, is very special because it has its own air. However, it is poisonous—not air that you could breathe. But as far as we know, no other moon in the solar system has any air at all.

The seventh planet, Uranus, is a greenish-blue gas giant with ten dark rings and about 15 small moons. Uranus is tiny compared to Saturn, but there would still be room for almost 70 Earths inside it.

Uranus is different from Saturn in another way as well. Both of the other gas giants, Jupiter and Saturn, stand up straight in space, with their rings around their middles. But Uranus lies on its side, so that the rings stand straight up.

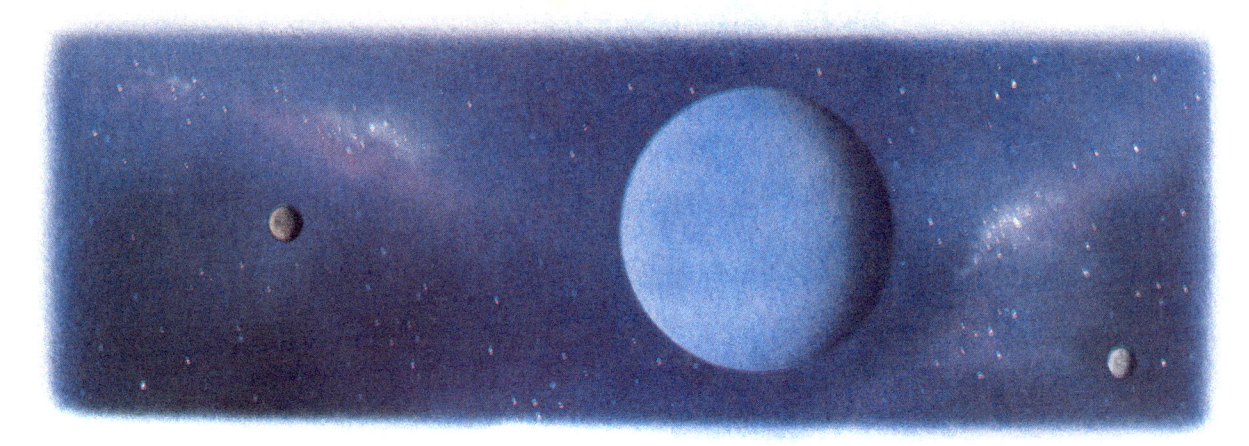

Neptune is the eighth planet and the last gas giant in the solar system. It is about the same size as Uranus and is pale blue in color.

Neptune is so far away that we know very little about it. But we do know that it has three moons, and it may be surrounded by rings as well.

The ninth and last planet in the solar system is Pluto. It is a little smaller than Earth's moon and is made of rock and ice, but mostly ice. Because it is far from the warming sun, Pluto is the coldest place in the solar system. Like Earth, Pluto has a moon of its own, called Charon.

Beyond Pluto there is little but darkness and stars. Each of those seemingly tiny stars is really a big bright sun like our sun. But they are so far away that they look like small points of light. The nearest star is 700 times farther from Pluto than cold little Pluto is from the sun.

If we are ever to explore these stars, we will need spaceships that can cross huge distances in the blink of an eye. We will need the kind of spaceships you only read about in books and see in movies today—the kind of spaceships that you may help build someday.